THE OFFICIAL BUS HANDBOOK

FOR BUS AND SCHOOL BUS DRIVERS

This handbook is only a guide. For official purposes, please refer to the Ontario Highway Traffic Act and regulations as well as the Public Vehicles Act and Regulations for official and legal information.

Professional drivers in Ontario can promote road safety by driving with skill and consideration for others.

Disponible en français
Demandez le «Guide officiel des autobus»

Driving is a privilege—not a right

Contents

Introduction

This handbook, along with the Driver's Handbook, is designed to help drivers apply for licences to operate buses and school buses: class B, C, E, or F driver's licences. It sets out the information you will need to know and the skills you will be expected to demonstrate in order to qualify for these licences.

As well as the rules of the road, bus drivers need to know the laws governing the operation of vehicles that transport passengers. They must have special driving skills and demonstrate safe driving practices that apply to those vehicles.

The handbook is divided into four sections. Section one contains information that applies to all vehicles that carry passengers. Section two offers information about licence classes C and F. Section three gives information about school buses. The last section is for reference and contains sections of the Highway Traffic Act and related regulations.

GETTING YOUR LICENCE

Legislation

These Acts and regulations govern certain aspects of the movement of passengers and goods, and the operation of vehicles.

1. The Highway Traffic Act (H.T.A.) and regulations govern the driver, the vehicle and equipment, weight and numbers of passengers that a bus driver can carry.
2. The Motor Vehicle Transport Act (Federal) regulates the for hire transportation of goods and people.
3. The Public Vehicles Act and regulations control the for hire movement of people on the highways by bus.

Licence Combinations

A driver may hold a class A, B, C, D, E, F, G, G1, G2, M, M1 or M2 driver's licence or combination. But a probationary, G1, G2, M, M1 or M2 driver may not hold a school bus driver's licence, (class B or E) or a driving instructor's licence.

There are several possible combinations of licences. For example, you can hold a class A and B if you meet the requirements for both. Your licence designation in this case would be shown as AB.

Any class or combination of licence classes from G to A may be combined with a class M licence authorizing the operation of motorcycles if you meet the requirements for class M. The combinations AM, EM, ABM and so on, are other examples of combinations.

Getting Your Licence

Higher Classes

Medical

When applying for a class A, B, C, D, E, or F licence, you must provide a completed ministry medical certificate. You can get blank medical forms from any MTO Driver Examination Office. A licence will be refused if your physical or medical condition does not meet the standards outlined in the regulations of the HTA.

If your licence is conditional on wearing corrective lenses, do not drive without wearing them. Your medical practitioner or optometrist is required by law to report to the licensing authorities any health problems that might affect your safe operation of a motor vehicle.

Defensive Driving

The most important concern to a bus driver is the safety of the passengers. Professional drivers who carry passengers must observe the rules of the road; understand and practice defensive driving; and take special precautions in loading and unloading.

The professional looks ahead, thinks ahead, acts early and drives defensively.

A person who drives defensively:

1. Keeps space around the vehicle;
2. Keeps his or her eyes moving and sees what is happening far ahead and to the sides;
3. Checks the mirrors frequently;
4. Recognizes possible danger far enough in advance to take preventive action smoothly, with a margin for error;
5. Makes allowances for the errors of other drivers and pedestrians;
6. Gives up the right-of-way if it will avoid possible danger to yourself or passengers;
7. Makes allowance for the rapidly changing conditions of the road, weather and traffic;
8. Shows courtesy to other road users;
9. Wears a seat belt and when seat belts are installed, ensures that passengers are buckled in;
10. Uses headlights at all times to make sure the bus is easily seen.
11. Drives at a safe speed, slowing when road conditions call for longer stopping distance and greater control.

Driving Techniques

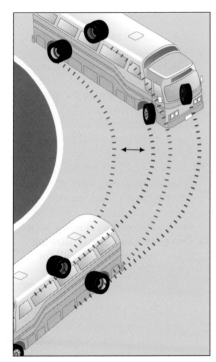

Diagram 1-1

Steering (Forward) and Off Track

The rear wheels of the vehicle do not pivot and so will not follow the same path as the front wheels. The greater the distance (wheel base) between the front wheels and the rear wheels of the vehicle, the greater the amount of "off-track". The off track path of the rear wheels is closer to the curb than the path of the front wheels.

On the highway, you must lead your turning arc of the front wheels according to the sharpness of the curve and your vehicle's off track. On a curve to the right keep the front wheels close to the centre line to prevent dropping the rear wheels off the pavement. On a curve to the left, keep the front wheels closer to the right edge of the pavement to prevent the rear wheels from crossing into the other traffic lane.

Whenever possible, make turns from the proper lanes. When you must use portions of another lane to make sharp turns, it is your responsibility to be sure that such a move can be made safely, without interfering with other traffic.

Steering While Reversing

When backing, use all rear view mirrors. Back slowly even with two or three mirrors, because your vision to the rear is limited. There is always a blind spot to the rear that a mirror cannot reflect.

When you have no observer, you should leave the vehicle and check the path that it will take.

Driving Techniques

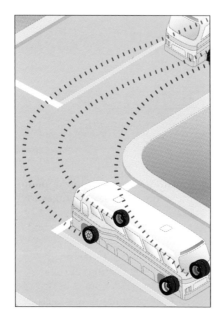

Diagram 1-2

Right Turns

Right turns with vehicles that have a lot of off track, require the driver to lead the turning arc according to the amount of off track. Running the rear wheels of the unit over curbs and sidewalks is dangerous and will also damage your tires. Power poles, sign posts or lamp standards mounted close to the curbing at intersections are fixed object hazards.

Generally, it is better to use more space from the road you are leaving than to use more space from the road you are entering.

In narrow streets, proceed well into the intersection before turning the steering wheel. You may need to travel partially over the centre line of the street entered or into the second traffic lane. If so, you must use extreme caution and make sure you can move safely.

When you have to "block" off another traffic lane, make sure that smaller vehicles such as motorcycles and bicycles are not moving up on your right side. Remember, your ability to see is restricted when you are in the middle of a turn.

Diagram 1-3

Left Turns

Be aware of any off tracking when making a left turn. Unless you use your left outside mirror to monitor the path of the rear wheels, those wheels may hit a vehicle or a sign post on an island. You must turn the vehicle in a wide arc before bringing it back to its proper position after a left turn, just right of the centre line.

Then as you speed up, you can move, when it is safe, to the right lane.

Brake Inspection

While you are not expected to be able to repair your brakes, you should be able to tell when there is a problem. Use the following inspection routine as part of your daily trip inspection.

1. Hydraulic brakes (without power assist):
   a. apply brakes moderately and hold;
   b. if the pedal shows a steady drop, the vehicle should be taken out of service and the system inspected professionally.
2. Hydraulic brakes (with power assist):
   a. with the engine stopped, pump the brake pedal several times to eliminate power assist;
   b. apply brakes moderately and hold;
   c. start the engine (the pedal should drop slightly) and stop;
   d. if the pedal continues to drop or does not drop (no power assist) stop the engine. The vehicle should be taken out of service and the system inspected professionally.

Driving Techniques

Use of Brakes

1. Apply brakes with steady pressure at the beginning of a stop, then ease off as the vehicle slows. Just before the vehicle comes to a complete stop, release brakes to avoid jerk and rebound, then brake again to hold the vehicle while stopped.
2. Hydraulic brakes or air brakes should not be fanned (alternately applied and released) except on slippery pavement where this type of braking may give better control, reduce the danger of skidding and give a shorter stop. However, fanning air brakes may sharply reduce air pressure. Fanning serves no useful purpose on dry pavement and on a long downhill grade may reduce air pressure below the minimum pressure needed for stopping the vehicle.
3. Avoid excessive use of brakes on long downgrades as overheated brakes are dangerously inefficient. Gear down to use engine compression as the principal means of controlling speed on long grades. You should use the same gear going down a long grade as you would to climb it. Choose the lower gear before you begin going downhill.
4. If the low air pressure warning device operates at anytime, stop immediately in the safest available place and have the problem corrected before you proceed.
5. If your brakes fail on a level road, down-shift (manual or automatic) and use engine compression to slow the vehicle. In an emergency, it may be necessary to use the emergency brake. Do not drive the vehicle again until repairs have been made.
6. Take care when braking on a wet or slippery surface or on a curve. Late or over-braking in these circumstances could cause skidding. To stop a skid, release the brakes, look and steer in the direction you want to go.

Following Distance

Commercial motor vehicles must keep a minimum distance of at least 60 m (200 feet) between themselves and other vehicles when on a highway at a speed over 60 km/h (40 mph.) except when overtaking and passing another vehicle.

NOTE: IF YOU PLAN TO OPERATE A VEHICLE EQUIPPED WITH AIR BRAKES, REFER TO THE AIR BRAKE HANDBOOK FOR MORE INFORMATION.

Special Precautions

1. Starting and stopping a vehicle should be a smooth, gradual operation. With a manual transmission, use the hand brake to hold the vehicle while co-ordinating the clutch and accelerator. This helps prevent rolling back on an upgrade. Thinking ahead can eliminate the need for sudden stops.

2. Bad weather requires all drivers to adjust their driving habits and take extra care. Noise, worries and other distractions slow down a driver's ability to react. Slow down and keep more clear space around the vehicle.
A vehicle with manual (standard) transmission and conventional tires may start a great deal easier on glare ice if you place the gear selector lever in second gear.

3. Think ahead and prepare for hazards such as narrow or rough roads, sharp turns, narrow bridges, and severe dust - slow down.

4. Ventilate and heat the vehicle when necessary.

5. Close and secure all doors when the vehicle is moving.

6. Never permit an unauthorized person to sit in the driver's seat, operate the vehicle, or any of its controls.

7. Do not allow passengers to obstruct the vision of the driver to the front, sides or rear.

8. Never load the vehicle beyond its licensed capacity. (Transit buses operate over seated capacity with no limits on standees.)

9. Except when passing, keep 60 m (200 ft) between buses travelling in the same direction on a highway outside a city, town or village.

Stall or Breakdown Procedure

If the vehicle stalls or breaks down on the highway, quickly and calmly act to protect the passengers and other motorists.

1. Stop as far off the roadway as possible.

2. If you cannot find and repair the trouble, remain with the vehicle and ask a responsible person to find help.

3. Set out appropriate flares, lamps, lanterns or portable reflectors as required by the Highway Traffic Act at a distance of approximately 30 metres (100 feet) in advance of the vehicle and 30 metres (100 feet) to the rear. They must be visible from 150 metres (500 feet) in each direction.

Special Precautions

What to Do in Case of a Collision:

1. Immediately stop and investigate;
2. Turn off the ignition and check for fire. There should be no smoking or open flame near the vehicle;
3. Set out warning flares or reflectors immediately;
4. Do first aid or call for an ambulance, if necessary. Call the police if there have been personal injuries or property damage of more than $700;
5. Collect the information you will need for a complete and detailed report of the collision and give other parties, witnesses, or police who ask for them, your name and address; the name and address of the vehicle owner and the vehicle permit number.

Fires

There are three common causes of vehicle fires:

1. leaking fuel;
2. electrical shorts;
3. overheated brakes.

Every driver should know how to use a fire extinguisher.

Remember in case of fire:

1. Remove passengers from the vehicle quickly and in an orderly manner;
2. Direct passengers to a safe place.

BUS LICENCE CLASSES C AND F

A class C licence is needed to drive any bus with seats for more than twenty-four (24) passengers, but not a school purposes bus carrying passengers. It allows the driver to operate vehicles included in classes D, F and G, but not motorcycles.

A class F licence is needed to drive any ambulance or any bus with seats for ten (10) or more passengers, but not more than twenty-four (24) passengers, and not a school purposes bus carrying passengers. It also allows the driver to operate vehicles included in class G, but not motorcycles.

Definitions

Here are definitions of some words used in this section.

Highway: a common and public highway, street, avenue, parkway, driveway, square, place, bridge, viaduct or trestle, any part of which is used by the public for the passage of vehicles, including the shoulders of the road and the land between property lines.

Roadway: the part of the highway that is improved, designed or ordinarily used for traffic, not including the shoulder. Where a highway includes two or more separate roadways, the term roadway refers to any one roadway and not all of the roadways together.

Bus: a motor vehicle designed and used for carrying ten or more passengers.

Qualification Requirements for Classes C and F

Regular Passenger Bus or Coach and/or Ambulance

There are two classes of licences for drivers of regular passenger buses, determined by the seating capacity of the bus. There is also a licence class for driving an ambulance or any bus with seats for 10 or more passengers, but not more than 24 passengers and not a school purposes bus carrying passengers.

An applicant for a class "C" or "F" driver's licence must:

1. be at least 18 years of age;
2. meet medical and vision standards;
3. have knowledge of bus equipment maintenance and passenger safety and control;
4. pass an MTO driver examination or obtain a certificate of competence from a recognized authority by passing a vision screening, knowledge test, and a driving test in a vehicle of appropriate size.

How to Obtain a Class C or F Driver's Licence

1. Pick up the necessary forms from any MTO Driver Examination Office, including the application, medical examination report, and study material.
2. Take the medical report to a physician of your choice. When the medical report has been completed, return it to the MTO examination office selected for your tests. If the medical report is satisfactory, you can make an appointment for your test.
3. You will be required to pass the following tests:
   a. a vision screening;
   b. traffic signs recognition test;
   c. a test of operating knowledge for a bus or an ambulance;
   d. a driving test in a vehicle with an appropriate number of seats;
   e. a satisfactory driver record search.

Road Tests

During your road test you will be asked to demonstrate:
1. a daily trip inspection known as a circle check. You will name the item of equipment checked and briefly describe its condition.
2. You will be required to drive in traffic and handle the vehicle safely according to the class of licence for which you are applying.
3. You may be required to reverse the vehicle into a parking bay or marked area.

Daily Trip Inspection, Classes C and F

Diagram 2-1

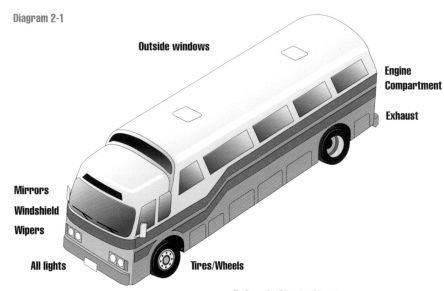

Outside windows

Engine Compartment

Exhaust

Mirrors

Windshield

Wipers

All lights

Tires/Wheels

Note: If the vehicle is being used as a school purposes vehicle, the daily trip inspection used will be the one on pages 24 to 26, for school purposes vehicles.

the condition of the vehicle can change. By staying alert, you can spot trouble before it causes a breakdown or collision.

Outside inspection

1. headlights, turn signals, parking and clearance lights;
2. windshield and wipers;
3. engine compartment: fluid levels, wiring, belts and hoses;
4. tires;
5. exposed wheel nuts, lugs and studs;
6. exhaust system (check for leaks);
7. stop, tail and hazard lights;
8. emergency exits;
9. rear windows (check for cleanliness) if applicable;
10. entrance door;
11. body condition (check for sharp edges);
12. fuel system (check for leaks);

Driver's Circle Check

All drivers must, by law, make a thorough stationary and operating inspection of their vehicle every day. They must continue to check all systems throughout the day because

The Daily Road Check

Inside inspection

1. steering wheel (for too much freeplay);
2. brake pedal reserve and fade;
3. brake booster operation;
4. brake failure warning light;
5. parking brake operation;
6. brake air pressure or vacuum gauge;
7. warning signal, low air pressure/vacuum gauge;
8. turn indicator and hazard lights, switch and pilot;
9. interior lights;
10. windshield washer fluid light;
11. windshield and windows;
12. mirrors, adjustment and condition;
13. defroster and heaters;
14. horn;
15. driver's seat belt and seat security;
16. emergency equipment.

(While driving the vehicle)
Plan a road check to evaluate your vehicle's steering, suspension, clutch, transmission, driveline and other components. It will help determine whether the engine performs properly, and whether the brakes have enough stopping power.

You can do a road check on the way to pick up the first passengers of the day.

Engine Check:

Be alert for any unusual engine noises, vibrations or lack of normal responses.

Test Parking Brake:

To check this brake, try to move the vehicle forward slowly while the parking brake is on. If it moves easily, the parking brake is not holding properly and should be repaired.

Check Transmission Operation:

A manual transmission should allow for smooth, easy gear changes.

Standard Transmission - Check Clutch

When starting an engine, the clutch pedal should be depressed to relieve the starter of the extra load of turning the transmission gears. The clutch should engage easily and smoothly without jerking, slipping excessively or chattering. Never "ride" the clutch pedal. A properly adjusted clutch pedal should have some freeplay when the pedal is fully released.

While changing gears, carefully control the speed of the engine to shift without jerking or excessive clutch slippage. Erratic or careless gear shifting wears out the clutch.

Note: Driving with the parking brake on is the most frequent cause of parking brake failure.

17

The Daily Road Check

Check the Brakes:

Test your brakes at low speeds, bringing the vehicle to a complete stop in a straight line. There should be no pulling to one side or excessive noise. Note any extra pedal pressure needed, or sponginess of the pedal. Do not drive the vehicle until problems have been repaired. If your vehicle is equipped with air brakes, please refer to The Air Brake Handbook.

Check the Steering:

Look for jerking or too much play in the system. Power steering should be quiet, and the vehicle should steer easily in turns or when going over bumps. Look for unusual ride or handling.

Check the Suspension:

Broken springs, ruptured air bags and faulty shock absorbers may cause sag, bouncing, bottoming and excessive sway when driving.

Stay Alert to the Condition of Your Vehicle:

Drivers should quickly sense the "thump-thumping" of a flat tire, or one that is underinflated. Keep the right air pressure in the tires at all times to prevent premature tire wear, failure and breakdown. The air pressure in your spare tire should be the same as the pressure in the tire on the vehicle carrying the highest pressure. Again, recognize unusual noises or handling.

SCHOOL BUS LICENCE CLASSES B AND E

A class B licence is needed to drive any school purposes bus having seats for **more than** twenty-four (24) passengers. It also allows you to operate vehicles included in classes C, D, E, F and G, but not motorcycles.

A class E licence is needed to drive any school purposes bus having seats for **not more than** twenty-four (24) passengers. It also allows you to operate vehicles included in classes F and G, but not motorcycles.

Definitions

Here are definitions of some words used in this section.

Bus: a motor vehicle designed for carrying ten or more passengers and used for the transportation of persons.

A school purposes bus is:

a. a bus while being operated by or under contract with a school board or other authority in charge of a school for the transportation of adults with a developmental handicap or children, or

b. a school bus, as defined in subsection 175 (1) of the HTA while being used for the transportation of adults with a developmental handicap or children.

A school bus:

a. is painted chrome yellow, and
b. displays on the front and rear thereof the words "school bus" and on the rear thereof the words "do not pass when signals flashing".

A school purposes vehicle:

a. a station wagon, van or bus while being operated by or under contract with a school board or other authority in charge of a school for the transportation of adults with a developmental handicap or children, or,
b. a school bus as defined in subsection 175 (1) of the HTA.

Median strip: the portion of a highway that separates traffic travelling in one direction from traffic travelling in the opposite direction with a physical barrier or a raised or depressed paved or unpaved separation area that inhibits traffic between roadways.

Highway: a common and public highway, street, avenue, parkway, driveway, square, place, bridge, viaduct or trestle, any part of which is used by the public for the passage of vehicles, including the shoulders of the road and the land between property lines.

Roadway: the part of the highway that is improved, designed or ordinarily used for traffic, not including the shoulder. Where a highway includes two or more separate roadways, the term roadway refers to any one roadway and not all of the roadways together.

NOTE: If you plan to operate a school bus or bus equipped with air brakes, you wil need a Z endorsement on your licence. Please refer to the AIR BRAKE HANDBOOK for more information.

Qualification Requirements for Classes B and E

An applicant for a class B or E driver's licence must:
1. be at least 21 years of age;
2. meet medical and vision standards;
3. not be classed as a probationary or novice driver;
4. have successfully completed a driver improvement course approved by the Minister;
5. have knowledge of bus equipment maintenance and passenger safety and control;
6. pass an M.T.O. Driver Examination or obtain a certificate of competence from a recognized authority by passing a vision screening, knowledge test and a driving test in a bus of appropriate size;
7. not have accumulated more than six demerit points on his/her driving record;
8. not have had a driver's licence under suspension at any time within the preceding 12 months

as a result of having been convicted or found guilty of:
   a. driving under suspension;
   b. speeding over 50 km above the limit;
   c. careless driving;
   d. racing on a highway;
   e. leaving the scene of an accident;
   f. a Criminal Code of Canada offence; committed by means of a motor vehicle or while driving or having care and control of a motor vehicle;
   g. flight from police;
9. not have been convicted or found guilty within the preceding five years of two or more offences under the Criminal Code of Canada, committed on different dates by means of a motor vehicle, or while driving or having care and control of a motor vehicle;
10. not have been convicted or found guilty within the preceding five

years under section 4 or 5 of The Narcotic Control Act of Canada;
11. not have been convicted or found guilty within the preceding five years of certain sexual or morals offences under the Criminal Code of Canada;
12. not have been convicted or found guilty of any offence for conduct that affords reasonable grounds for believing that he will not properly perform his duties, or is not a proper person to have custody of children.

In addition, a holder of a class B or E driver's licence may not accumulate more than eight demerit points.

How to Obtain a Class B or E Driver's Licence

1. From any driver examination office, obtain a school bus driver's licence kit which includes application forms, a medical examination report form, and study material. Check the qualification requirements listed on page 21.
2. Take the medical report to a physician of your choice. When the medical examination has been completed, return the report to the examination office selected for your tests. Arrangements will be made for the time and date of your tests provided the medical report is satisfactory.
3. A criminal record search will be initiated when you pay your application fee.
4. You are required to pass the following:
   a. vision screening;
   b. traffic signs recognition test;
   c. test of operating knowledge for a bus or an ambulance;
   d. driving test in a vehicle of appropriate seating capacity;
   e. a satisfactory driver search record.

Road Tests

On your road test you will demonstrate:
1. a daily trip inspection, commonly known as a circle check. You will name the item of equipment checked and briefly describe its condition;
2. you will drive in traffic and handle the vehicle safely according to the class of licence for which you are applying;
3. loading and unloading;
4. you may be required to reverse the vehicle into a parking bay or marked area;
5. proper procedures at an unprotected railway crossing.

Daily Trip Inspection, Classes B and E

Driver's Circle Check

All drivers must, by law, make a thorough stationary and operating inspection of their vehicle every day. They must continue to check all systems throughout the day because the condition of the vehicle can change. Continued alertness will permit any driver to spot trouble before it results in a breakdown or collision.

The law requires a vehicle transporting six or more children to and from school and operated by or under contract with a school board or other authority in charge of a school, to be equipped with a log book.

(For more information, refer to section 4 of Regulation 612 - Page 38.)

You must also record the number of hours worked in an "hours of service" log book.

Diagram 3-1

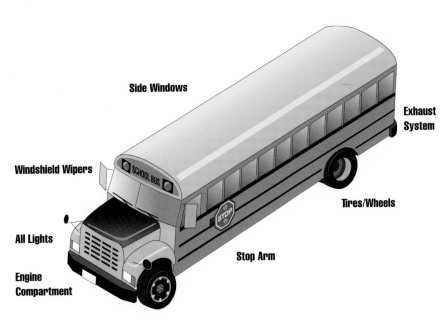

Side Windows

Exhaust System

Windshield Wipers

SCHOOL BUS

STOP

Tires/Wheels

All Lights

Stop Arm

Engine Compartment

Daily Trip Inspection, Classes B and E

Outside Inspection

1. Alternating lights, front;
2. Headlights, directional signals, parking and clearance lights;
3. Windshield and wipers;
4. Engine compartment: Fluid levels, wiring, belts and hoses;
5. Tires (retreads on rear wheels only);
6. Exposed wheel nuts, lugs and studs;
7. Exhaust system for leaks;
8. Directional, stop tail and clearance lights;
9. Emergency exit;
10. Alternating lights, rear;
11. Rear windows (for cleanliness) if applicable;
12. Entrance door;
13. Body condition (for sharp edges);
14. Fuel system (for leaks);
15. Signs (for cleanliness and legibility);
16. Stop Arm.

Diagram 3-2

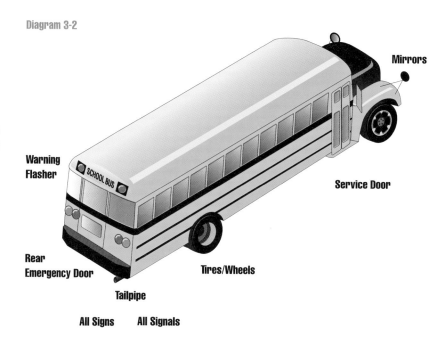

Mirrors

Warning Flasher

Service Door

Rear Emergency Door

Tires/Wheels

Tailpipe

All Signs   All Signals

Inside Inspection

1. Steering wheel (for excessive freeplay);
2. Brake pedal reserve and fade;
3. Brake booster operation;
4. Brake failure warning light;
5. Parking brake operation;
6. Brake air pressure or vacuum gauge;
7. Warning signal, low air pressure/vacuum;
8. Interior (for exhaust fumes);
9. Signal and hazard lights, switch and pilot;
10. Alternating lights, switch and signal device;
11. Interior lights;
12. Windshield washer and lights;
13. Windshield and windows;
14. Mirrors, adjustment and condition;
15. Defroster and heaters;
16. Horn;
17. Stop arm mechanism;
18. Driver's seat belt and seat security;
19. Service door and controls;
20. Passengers' seat security;
21. Emergency exit and warning signal;
22. Floor covering (tripping hazards);
23. Fire extinguisher;
24. Axe or claw bar;
25. First aid kit;
26. Flares, fuzees or reflectors;
27. Interior (for cleanliness);
28. Passenger seat belts (if so equipped).

Final Check before Driving Onto the Highway:

1. Driver's seat belt fastened;
2. Drive forward and brake to a stop to test the service brake;
3. Additional check of all gauges - heat, oil and vacuum, etc.;
4. Complete log book entry.

NOTE: If this type of vehicle is being used for other than a school purposes vehicle, the daily trip inspection used will be the one on pages 16 and 17 for coaches.

The Daily Road Check

(While driving the vehicle)
Plan a road check to evaluate your vehicle's steering, suspension, clutch, transmission, driveline and other components to determine whether the engine performs properly, and whether the brakes have enough stopping power.

You can do a road check on the way to pick up the first passengers of the day.

Engine Check:
Be alert for any unusual engine noises, vibrations or lack of normal responses.

NOTE: Driving with the parking brake on is the most frequent cause of parking brake failure.

Test Parking Brake:
To check this brake, try to move the vehicle forward slowly while the parking brake is on. If it moves easily, the parking brake is not holding properly and should be repaired.

Check Transmission Operation:
A manual transmission should allow for smooth, easy gear changes.

Standard Transmission - Check Clutch:
The clutch should engage easily and smoothly without jerking, slipping excessively or chattering. Never "ride" the clutch pedal. A properly adjusted clutch pedal should have some "freeplay" when the pedal is fully released.

While changing gears, carefully control the speed of the engine to shift without jerking or excessive clutch slippage. Erratic or careless gear shifting wears out the clutch.

Check the Brakes:
Test at low speeds, bringing the vehicle to a complete stop. The vehicle should stop in a straight line. There should be no pulling to one side or excessive noise. Note any extra pedal pressure or sponginess. Do not operate the vehicle until such conditions have been repaired.

Check the Steering:
Look for jerking or excessive play in the system. Power steering should be quiet, and the vehicle should steer easily in turns or when going over bumps. Look for unusual ride or handling.

Check the Suspension:
Broken springs, ruptured air bags and faulty shock absorbers may cause sag, bouncing, bottoming and excessive sway when under way.

Loading and Unloading

Stay Alert to the Condition of Your Vehicle:

Drivers should quickly sense the "thump-thumping" of a flat tire, or one that is underinflated. Keep the right air pressure in the tires to prevent premature tire wear, failure and breakdown. The air pressure in your spare tire should be the same as the pressure in the tire on the vehicle carrying the highest pressure. Again, recognize unusual noises or handling.

Loading and unloading are critical operations and may be dangerous unless they are done carefully.

The driver must turn on the upper alternating red signal lights before stopping to load or unload. As soon as the bus is stopped, the driver must extend the school bus stop arm. The school bus must remain stopped with the lights flashing and the stop arm extended until all passengers who must cross the highway have completed the crossing.

The law applies everywhere, regardless of the posted speed limit - on highways, county roads, city, town or village streets. Motorists meeting a stopped school bus with upper alternating red signal lights flashing must stop unless they are on a highway divided by a median strip. Motorists overtaking a stopped school bus with upper alternating red signal lights flashing on any highway must always stop at least

20 metres behind the bus. In both cases, motorists may not proceed until the bus moves, or the lights have stopped flashing.

The fine for failing to stop when required is $200 to $1,000 for a first offence; for each subsequent offence $500 to $2,000, or imprisonment for up to six months, or both. In every case, the driver will be given six demerit points.

When loading or unloading at traffic signal lights, the driver must **not** activate the upper alternating red flashing lights and stop arm on the school bus. The stop should be made as close as possible to the intersection, close to the curb or edge of the roadway and the passengers cautioned to obey the traffic signal lights.

If a driver needs to stop near an intersection with traffic signal lights and use the flashing red lights and stop arm, the stop should be made at

27

least 60 m from the intersection.

At a school bus loading zone, the driver must stop the school bus close to the right curb or edge of the roadway between the signs setting out the limits of the zone. Within this zone, the flashing lights and arm must **not** be operated. Buses must not stop to load or unload on the opposite side of the highway from a school bus loading zone.

The school bus stopping law only applies to chrome yellow school buses with proper markings and signals as defined in Section 175 of the Highway Traffic Act and only when loading or unloading children or adults with a developmental handicap. Drivers of other school purposes vehicles must realize they do not have the protection of this law. They must be very careful in choosing places to stop and directing their passengers as they leave the bus.

The driver should make sure that the following rules are observed:
1. passengers should not be loaded or unloaded on a steep grade or curve. There should be a clear view of the road in each direction for at least 150 m (500 feet);
2. entering the bus, passengers should go directly to their seats and sit down before the bus moves;
3. passengers should stay seated until the bus has come to a full stop;
4. passengers should not enter or leave the bus while it is moving;
5. passengers should not be allowed to obstruct the vision of the driver to the front, sides or rear;
6. the school bus should stop on the travelled portion of the roadway and not the shoulder to load or unload passengers;
7. passengers leaving the vehicle should cross only in front of the bus and approximately three

metres (10 feet) from the front;
8. when more than one student leaves the bus, students should form a group approximately three metres (10 feet) from the front of the bus and on the right shoulder or curb of the road;
9. the group of passengers should look for the driver's signal indicating it is safe to cross;
10. passengers who remain on the right side of the stopped bus, should form a group and stay together, away from the front right corner of the bus until the bus moves away;
11. before crossing, passengers should look both ways before stepping into the roadway and continue to watch for traffic;
12. passengers should always cross the roadway at right angles to the bus, never diagonally;
13. passengers should walk, never run, when crossing the roadway.

Special Precautions for School Buses

1. Starting and stopping a vehicle should be a smooth, gradual operation. With a manual transmission, use the hand brake to hold the vehicle while co-ordinating the clutch and accelerator. This helps prevent rolling back on an upgrade. Thinking ahead can eliminate the need for sudden stops.

2. Bad weather requires all drivers to adjust their driving habits and take extra care. Noise, worries and other distractions slow down a driver's ability to react. Slow down and keep more clear space around the vehicle.
   A vehicle with manual (standard) transmission and conventional tires may start a great deal easier on glare ice if you place the gear selector lever in second gear.

3. Think ahead and prepare for hazards such as narrow or rough roads, sharp turns, narrow bridges, and severe dust - slow down.

4. Ventilate and heat the vehicle when necessary.

5. When the vehicle is moving, the doors should be safely closed, but must not be locked.

6. Never permit an unauthorized person to sit in the driver's seat, operate the vehicle, or any of its controls.

7. Do not allow passengers to obstruct the vision of the driver to the front, sides or rear.

8. Never load the vehicle beyond its licensed capacity.

9. Except when passing, keep 60 m (200 ft) between buses travelling in the same direction on a highway outside a city, town or village.

10. No lunch pails, books or parcels should be in the aisles or step wells, at any time.

11. Use care and caution when you are backing a bus. Drivers should use the rear view mirror, turn and look back and have someone give directions. Back slowly and cautiously, and watch traffic conditions around the vehicle at all times. Drivers should not back up their vehicles on school grounds or at loading or unloading stops or zones without proper guidance and signals from a responsible person outside the bus.

12. School buses and public transit vehicles must stop at least five metres (15 feet) from the nearest rail at all railway crossings. While stopped, the driver must open the bus door and look and listen for any approaching trains. The driver must not change gears when the bus is actually crossing the tracks. The flashing lights and stop arm must not be activated in this situation.

13. When stopped, waiting at an intersection or railway crossing, it is a safe practice to place the gearshift lever in neutral and release the clutch. At a railway crossing, set the parking brake, as well.

14. Never leave the vehicle without first stopping the engine, setting the brakes, putting the transmission on its lowest gear or park position and removing the ignition key.

15. "Spotters" or safety patrollers may help the school bus driver when loading or unloading a school bus. The spotter can prevent the driver from accidentally driving over and killing or injuring a child who stopped in a blind area in front of the vehicle. Recently developed safety equipment includes newly designed mirrors or multiple mirror adjustment systems, motion detector systems, bumper-mounted crossing barriers, and perimeter braking systems. When drivers and passengers are trained to use them effectively, they will enhance safety.

16. When a school bus is disabled on a roadway when lights are required, flares or reflectors must be placed 30 m (100 ft) in front and behind the vehicle.

Emergency Procedures for School Buses

There is a potential for disaster in school busing. It is important that you and your passengers know how to get out of the bus using the emergency exits, and use of the safety equipment.

It is your responsibility to set up routine evacuation practice. In an emergency, practice can mean an orderly and speedy evacuation even if you are injured and unable to help. This practice should take place at the beginning of the school year and every month afterwards.

Coordinate practice drills with the school administration and hold your drills in a safe, traffic-free area on school property.

Evacuation Procedure

The objective is to get the children off the bus safely in the shortest possible time and in an orderly way.

Here are three standard ways to evacuate a school bus:

a. Through the front exit only;
b. Through the rear exit only:
c. Through the front and rear exits simultaneously.

The push out windows can be used for exiting in an extreme situation.

Procedure

1. Assess the situation. Generally, the quickest method is to use both front and rear doors. If those exits expose people to other dangers such as fire or traffic, choose the safest exit.
2. Remain calm. Speak loudly, but slowly. Ask the passengers to move calmly to the exit you choose.
3. Assign a responsible leader to count the passengers as they leave and lead them to a safe area away from the bus. The leader should keep everyone together.
4. Assign some taller students to wait at the rear exit on the ground at either side of the door to help as the students swing down. Another student inside tells the exiting person to "watch your head; put your hands on the helper's shoulders and swing down".
5. While the other students remain in their seats, the students closest to danger should leave one seat at a time by walking to the exit.
6. All articles such as lunches, books, and so on, should be left behind.
7. As the last person leaves, walk the length of the bus to be sure everyone is out and then exit yourself. Begin first aid treatment if necessary. Assign two responsible students to go for help if needed and organize helpers to put out warning flares or reflectors as required.

Practice cannot eliminate all injury, but it will certainly reduce the possibility of unnecessary injury to yourself, your passengers and other motorists.

Care and Maintenance of the School Bus

Mechanical Fitness of School Purposes Vehicles:

Regulations under the Highway Traffic Act require regular inspection of every station wagon, van, or bus operated by or under contract to a school board or other authority in charge of a school for the transportation of:

a. six or more adults with a developmental handicap;

b. six or more children; or,

c. six or more persons referred to in a and b, between their homes and schools. Inspections are also required for a chrome yellow school bus transporting children between their homes and churches or adults with a developmental handicap between their homes and training centres.

These vehicles must display valid inspection sticker(s).

The inspection must be carried out in a licensed motor vehicle inspection station. Authorized inspection mechanics perform the inspection and affix stickers to vehicles found to be satisfactory.

A Clean School Bus:

The driver should keep the vehicle clean. Passengers will take pride in a bus that is neat and clean, and will cooperate in keeping it that way.

Daily Cleaning Routine:

The floor should be swept, seats dusted and inspected for damage and breakage. The side windows, windshield and mirrors should be cleaned, along with lights and reflectors.

Weekly Cleaning Routine:

Floors and seats should be washed. The exterior should be washed and the paint inspected. Door hinges and operating mechanisms should be oiled and checked.

School Bus Routes

The owner and driver of a school bus should be thoroughly familiar with the area. When route layouts are considered, the driver should help make recommendations to the school board, parents and where applicable, the vehicle owner. The best planned route is the safest. Information on the route should be available to everyone affected by the service.

Consider these factors when laying out routes and planning schedules:
1. age, health and physical condition of the passengers;
2. condition of the roads to be travelled;
3. school schedule;
4. distances between homes and school;
5. distances between homes and routes;
6. safety of walking routes between homes and routes;
7. number and size of available buses;
8. number of passengers to be served;
9. size of area;
10. location of bus stops;
11. seasonal conditions (such as snow banks);
12. location of safe turn-around points.

In choosing a route:
1. examine bad curves, steep hills, rough roads, narrow bridges, railroad crossings and other hazards;
2. make sure bus stops are free from physical hazards;
3. route buses as near to the homes of passengers as traffic, time and convenience permit;
4. where possible, pick up and drop off passengers on the home side of the road, to eliminate or reduce the number of passengers forced to cross the road;
5. prepare and follow a time schedule;
6. make sure turn-around points are safe in all weather, with firm traction and good visibility of oncoming traffic.

LAWS AND REGULATIONS

Highway Traffic Act - Law Relating to School Buses

Section 174

(1) The driver of:

(a) a bus, when transporting children to and from school; or

(b) a public vehicle, upon approaching on a highway a railway crossing that is not protected by gates or railway crossing signal lights or unless otherwise directed by a flagman shall stop such a vehicle not less than 5 m (15') from the nearest rail of the railway and, having stopped, shall look in both directions along the track and open a door of the vehicle and listen for any approaching train and, when it is safe to do so, shall cross the railway track in a gear that he will not have to change while crossing the track and he shall not change gears while crossing.

Section 175

In this section, "children" means:

(a) persons under the age of eighteen, and

(b) in the case where a school bus is being operated by or under a contract with a school board or other authority in charge of a school for the transportation of children to or from school includes students of the school;

"developmental handicap" means a condition of mental impairment, present or occurring during a person's formative years, that is associated with limitations in adaptive behavior,

NOTE: The penalty is a fine of not less than $60 and not more than $500.

Laws and Regulations

"school" does not include a post-secondary school educational institution;

"school bus" means a bus that:
(a) is painted chrome yellow, and
(b) displays on the front and rear thereof the words "school bus" and on the rear thereof the words "do not pass when signals flashing".

(2) For the purposes of subsection (3), a motor vehicle shall be deemed to be a bus if it is or has been operated under the authority of a permit for which a bus registration or validation fee was paid in any jurisdiction.

(3) No bus, except a bus that at any time during its current validation period is used to transport children or to transport adults who have developmental handicaps, shall be painted chrome yellow.

(4) No motor vehicle on a highway, other than a school bus, shall have displayed thereon the words "school bus" or the words "do not pass when signals flashing" or be equipped with a school bus stop arm.

(5) No person shall drive or operate a motor vehicle on a highway that contravenes subsection (3) or (4).

(6) Subject to subsection (9), every school bus driver:
(a) who is about to stop on a highway for the purpose of receiving or discharging children or receiving or discharging adults who have developmental handicaps, shall actuate the overhead red signal-lights on the bus;
(b) as soon as the bus is stopped for a purpose set out in clause (a), shall actuate the school bus stop arm; and
(c) while the bus is stopped for a purpose set out in clause (a) on a highway that does not have a median strip shall continue to operate the overhead red signal-lights and stop arm until all passengers having to cross the highway have completed the crossing.

(7) Clause 170 (1) (a) does not apply to a driver who stops in accordance with subsection (6).

(8) No person shall actuate the overhead red signal-lights or the stop arm on a school bus on a highway under any circumstances other than those set out in subsection (6).

(9) No person shall actuate the overhead red signal-lights or the stop arm on a school bus:
(a) at an intersection controlled by an operating traffic control signal system;
(b) at any other location controlled by an operating traffic control signal system at:
    i: a sign or roadway marking

indicating where the stop is to be made;

ii) the area immediately before entering the nearest crosswalk, if there is no sign or marking indicating where the stop is to be made; or

iii) a point not less than five metres before the nearest traffic control signal, if there is no sign, marking or crosswalk; or

(c) within sixty metres from a location referred to in clause (a) or (b).

(10) No person shall stop a school bus on a highway for the purpose of receiving or discharging children or receiving or discharging adults who have developmental handicaps;

(a) opposite a designated school bus loading zone; or

(b) at a designated school bus loading zone, except as close as practicable to the right curb or edge of the roadway.

(11) Every driver or street car operator, when meeting on a highway, other than a highway with a median strip, a stopped school bus that has its overhead red signal-lights flashing, shall stop before reaching the bus and shall not proceed until the bus moves or the overhead red signal-lights have stopped flashing.

(12) Every driver or street car operator on a highway, when approaching from the rear a stopped school bus that has its overhead red signal-lights flashing, shall stop at least twenty metres before reaching the bus and shall not proceed until the bus moves or the overhead red signal-lights have stopped flashing.

(13) A council of a municipality may be by-law designate school bus loading zones, in accordance with the regulations, on highways under its jurisdiction and, where it does so, subsection (6) does not apply to a driver about to stop or stopping in a zone so designated.

(14) No by-law passed under subsection (13) becomes effective until the highways or portions thereof affected have signs erected in compliance with this Act and the regulations.

(15) The Lieutenant Governor in Council may make regulations:

(a) respecting the operation of vehicles used for transporting children or for transporting adults who have developmental handicaps;

(b) prescribing the type, design and colour of vehicles referred to in clause (a) and the markings to be displayed thereon;

(c) requiring the use of any equipment on or in vehicles referred to in clause (a) and pre-

Laws and Regulations

scribing the standards and specifications of such equipment;

(d) prescribing the qualifications of drivers of vehicles referred to in clause (a) and prohibiting the operation thereof by unqualified persons;

(e) requiring the inspection of vehicles referred to in clause (a);

(f) respecting the designation of school bus loading zones, the location thereof, the erection of signs and the placing of markings on highways;

(g) prescribing the books and records that shall be kept by persons who operate vehicles used for transporting children or for transporting adults who have developmental handicaps;

(h) requiring the retention of prescribed books and records within vehicles and prescribing the information to be contained and the entries to be recorded in the books or records.

(16) Any regulation made under subsection (15) may be general or particular in its application.

(17) Every person who contravenes subsection (11) or (12) is guilty of an offence and on conviction is liable:

(a) for a first offence, to a fine of not less than $200 and not more than $1,000; and

(b) for each subsequent offence, to a fine of not less than $500 and not more than $2,000 or to imprisonment for a term of not more than six months, or to both.

(18) An offence referred to in subsection (17) committed more than five years after a previous conviction for either of the offences referred to in subsection (17) is not a subsequent offence for the purpose of clause (17) (b).

Regulation 612

1.-(1) Every school bus as defined in subsection (175) (1) of the Act, (or while being operated by or under a contract with a school board or other authority in charge of a school for the transportation of children) shall:

(a) display the words "school bus" on the front and rear thereof placed as near as is practicable to the top of the vehicle in a clearly visible position in black letters at least 200 millimetres high with the lines forming the letters being at least 32 millimetres wide on a yellow background;

(b) display the words "do not pass when signals flashing" on the rear thereof placed below and as near as is practicable to the words "school bus" in a clearly visible position in black letters not less than 75 and not more than 125 millimetres high with the lines forming the letters having a width of not less than one-sixth of the height of the letters on a yellow background;

(c) be equipped with signal lights that have an effective illuminating area of at least 7740 square millimetres, that produce a light of an intensity that is clearly visible at a distance of at least 152 metres and that are attached and operated as follows:

i) Two signal lights shall be placed on the front of the bus in as high a position as is practicable and shall, when operating, alternately produce flashes of red light visible only from the front of the bus,

ii) Two signal lights shall be placed on the rear of the bus in as high a position as is practicable and as far apart as is practicable and shall, when operating, alternately produce flashes of red light visible only from the rear of the bus,

iii) The signal lights prescribed in paragraphs 1 and 2 shall be actuated by a control device accessible to the driver and equipped to give him a clear and unmistakable signal either visible or audible when the signal lights are operating;

(d) be equipped with a first aid kit, being a sturdy dust-proof metal or plastic container containing:

i) four packets each containing four hand cleansers and twelve gauze cleansing pads,

ii) 150, individually wrapped twenty-five-millimetre by seventy-five-millimetre, adhesive dressings,

iii) eight fifty-millimetre compress dressings,

iv) six 100-millimetre compress dressings,

v) two eye dressing kits each containing one eye shield and two gauze pads,

vi) three four-ply gauze dressings at least 900 millimetres square,

vii) two fifty-millimetre by 5.5-metre gauze bandages,

viii) one packet of twenty-five-millimetre by 4.6-metre adhesive tape,

ix) six triangular bandages,

x) one seventy-millimetre by 610-millimetre rolled metal splint,

xi) one pair of scissors,

xii) one pair of sliver tweezers, and

xiii) twelve fifty-millimetre safety pins.

(e) in the case of a school bus

Laws and Regulations

manufactured on or after the 1st day of September, 1975, having a seating capacity for twenty-four or more passengers, be equipped with,
i) a convex cross-over mirror, at least 190 millimetres in diameter, securely mounted so that the seated driver may see the reflection of the are immediately in front of the front bumper of the bus, and
ii) a convex right front sideview mirror, securely mounted on the roof, right windshield corner post or exterior right rear-view mirror so that the seated driver may observe the reflection of the ground surface immediately adjacent to the right front wheel of the bus.
(f) in the case of a school bus manufactured on or after the 1st day of September, 1975, having a seating capacity for twenty-four or more passengers, have:
i) the chassis and the front bumper painted black; and
ii) the hood, grill and outside surfaces that are in direct line with the seated driver's vision painted lusterless black; and
(g) in the case of a school bus manufactured on or after the 1st day of December 1982, have:
i) the chassis and the front bumper painted black; and
ii) the hood grill and outside surfaces that are in direct line with the seated driver's vision painted lusterless black.
1.-(2) On and after the 1st day of September, 1983, every school bus referred to in subsection (1) shall be equipped with a stop arm device that complies with the requirements set out in subsection (3).
1.-(3) A stop arm device shall:
(a) be at least 450 millimetres high and 450 millimetres wide and octagonal in shape;
(b) display on the front and rear thereof the word "STOP" in white letters at least 150 millimetres high with the lines forming the letters being at least twenty millimetres wide on a red reflectorized background;
(c) be equipped with double-faced lamps located in the top and bottom portions of the stop arm, one above the other that are automatically activated so as to produce alternating flashes of red light, visible to the front and rear of the bus at the commencement of the stop arm cycle and deactivated when the stop arm is retracted;
(d) be installed on the left outside of the bus body and be mounted so as to be readily

seen by motorists approaching from the front or rear of the bus when the stop arm is in the extended position;

(e) operate automatically so as to move to the fully extended position when the service door of the bus is opened and return to the retracted position when the door is closed; and

(f) operate only when the alternating light circuit on the front and rear of the bus is energized.

1.-(4) In this regulation, "school purposes vehicle" means:

(a) a station wagon, van or bus while being operated by or under a contract with a school board or other authority in charge of a school for the transportation of adults with a developmental handicap or children; or

(b) a school bus as defined in subsection 175 of the Act.

2.-(1) No person shall sell or offer to sell a new school bus having a seating capacity for twenty-four or more passengers that has a body or chassis manufactured before the 1st day of September, 1987 and does not conform to the Canadian Standards Association Standard D250-M 1982 or D250-M 1985.

2.-(2) No person shall sell or offer to sell a new school bus that has a body and chassis manufactured on or after the 1st day of September, 1987 and does not conform to the Canadian Standards Association Standard D250-M 1985.

3.-(1) No bus shall be operated by or under contract to a school board or other authority in charge of a school to transport adults with a developmental handicap or children and no bus shall be operated unless,

(a) it is equipped with an interior mirror designed to provide the driver with a view of the passengers and two exterior rear view mirrors, one on the left and one on the right of the vehicle set to give the driver a clear view past the left rear and right rear of the vehicle;

(b) it is equipped with tire chains or snow tires for each driving wheel that is not of the dual type that are placed on the wheels when the conditions of the highway require their use;

(c) it is equipped with an accurate speedometer placed to indicate to the driver the speed of the vehicle at all times;

(d) it has a body floor constructed and insulated to prevent exhaust gases of the

Laws and Regulations

engine from entering the passenger compartment of the vehicle;

(e) it is equipped with two windshield wipers that operate at a constant speed and an effective defrosting device that provides clear vision through the windshield and the windows on the left and right sides of the driver;

(f) it is equipped with a light or lights arranged to provide light to the whole of the interior except the driver's position, and that are constantly lighted during darkness when there are passengers in the vehicle;

(g) it is equipped with an axe or clawbar and an adequate fire extinguisher both securely mounted in such a manner and place as to be readily accessible;

(h) it is equipped with depend-able tires that in the case of front tires have not been rebuilt;

(i) it is equipped with at least one door or exit and,

i) a door or exit for emergency use situated at the rear of the vehicle or near the rear on the left side of the vehicle and which has a door lock equipped with an interior handle which releases the lock when lifted up, or;

(ii) subject to subsection (2), at least three pushout windows on each side of the passenger compartment of the vehicle each of which,

(A) has a minimum height of 500 mm and a minimum width of 760 mm,

(B) is designed, constructed and maintained to open outwards when a reasonable amount of manual force is applied to the inside of the window, and

(C) displays on or adjacen to the window adequate directions for its emergency use.

3.-(2) A motor vehicle that is equipped in accordance with subclause 1 (i) (ii) shall be equipped with an additional pushout window located in the rear of the vehicle.

4.-(1) A school purpose vehicle while being operated for the transportation of six or more children, six or more adults with a developmental handicap or six or more persons from both categories shall be equipped with a log book containing the following information:

1. Vehicle identification number.
2. Vehicle make.
3. Model year of the vehicle.
4. A list of the items set out in Schedules 1 and 2.

4.-(2) The equipment and operating

characteristics of each vehicle referred to in subsection (1) shall be inspected by its driver each day that the vehicle is operated as described in subsection (1).

4.-(3) An inspection under subsection (2) shall include an inspection of the items set out in Schedules 1 and 2 if the vehicle is equipped with those items.

4.-(4) Where an inspection under subsection (2) reveals a defect, the driver shall forthwith report the defect to the person responsible for maintaining the vehicle.

4.-(5) Upon completing the inspection required by subsection (2), the driver shall record, in the log book referred to in subsection (1), the date of the inspection and any defects found on the inspection together with the name of the person to whom the defects were reported and shall sign the entry.

4.-(6) The person who repairs a defect reported under subsection (4) shall record in the appropriate log book the date on which the repair was completed and shall sign the entry.

5. Section 4 does not apply in respect of a bus operated by a municipality or a commission on behalf of a municipality,
(a) in regular transit service; or
(b) within the boundaries of the municipality.

School Purposes Vehicles

School Purposes Vehicles Inspection Reg. 611

10.-(1) A school purposes vehicle is prescribed as a type or class of vehicle to which section 85 of the Act applies while it is being used for the transportation of:
(a) six or more adults with a developmental handicap;
(b) six or more children; or
(c) six or more persons referred to in clause (a) or (b).

The Public Vehicles Act

23.-(1) No driver or operator shall allow passengers to ride on the fenders or any other part of a public vehicle other than the seats thereof except that a vehicle may carry as standing passengers in the aisles thereof not more than one-third the number of persons for which seats are provided.

Other Official Handbooks for You

Copies of this handbook and others may be purchased from a retail store near you, from a Driver Examination Office, from a Vehicle Licence Issuing Office or from the distributor.

Distribution:

General Publishing Co. Limited
325 Humber College Blvd.,
Etobicoke, Ontario
M9W 7C3

or by calling
(416) 213-1919 ext. 199
or 1 (800) 387-0141

Prepayment required by cheque or credit card — VISA or Mastercard

The Official Driver's Handbook $ 7.95
ISBN 0-7778-6141-0

The Official Motorcycle Handbook $ 7.95
ISBN 0-7778-6143-7

The Official Off-Road Vehicles Handbook $ 4.95
ISBN 0-7778-4456-7

The Official Truck Handbook $ 7.95
ISBN 0-7778-4454-0

The Official Bus Handbook $ 7.95
ISBN 0-7778-4452-4

The Official Air Brake Handbook $ 12.95
ISBN 0-7778-4450-8

All prices are subject to 7% G.S.T. and 5% Shipping Costs. Please add 12% to your total purchase to cover G.S.T. and shipping cost.

STOP! Did you know there are other books in the official driver information series?

Now you can purchase copies of this official handbook and five others from a retail store, a Driver Examination Office or a Vehicle Licence Issuing Office near you—or you can order them directly from the distributor.

Distribution: **General Publishing Co. Limited**
325 Humber College Blvd., Etobicoke, Ontario M9W 7C3
or by calling (416) 231-1919 ext. 199 or 1-800-387-0141 Fax (416) 213-1917

Prepayment required by cheque or credit card — VISA or Mastercard

QUANTITY		TOTAL
_____ ISBN 0-7778-6141-0 The Official Driver's Handbook	$ 7.95	_____
_____ ISBN 0-7778-6143-7 The Official Motorcycle Handbook	$ 7.95	_____
_____ ISBN 0-7778-4456-7 The Official Off-Road Vehicles Handbook	$ 4.95	_____
_____ ISBN 0-7778-4454-0 The Official Truck Handbook	$ 7.95	_____
_____ ISBN 0-7778-4452-4 The Official Bus Handbook	$ 7.95	_____
_____ ISBN 0-7778-4450-8 The Official Air Brake Handbook	$ 12.95	_____
	Sub-Total	_____
	Plus 12%	_____
	TOTAL	_____

All prices are subject to 7% G.S.T. and 5% Shipping Costs. Please add 12% to your total purchase to cover G.S.T. and shipping cost.

Payment by   cheque ☐   VISA ☐   Mastercard ☐

Credit Card No. _____ Expiry Date _____

Signature of Card Holder _____

SHIP TO (PLEASE PRINT):

Name: _____

Address: _____

Town/City: _____

Province: _____ Postal Code: _____

ONTARIO TRANSPORTATION MAP Series—including the Official Road Map of Ontario

Get a more detailed look at specific areas of Southern Ontario with this series of eight maps, scaled at 1:250,000. You'll find enlargements of major city centres, highways, townships, municipal roads including loose surface and seasonal roads, railways, airports, parks, O.P.P. detachments, hospitals, tourist attractions and service centres within each region.

Or pick up the Official Road Map of Ontario, which shows all of Ontario's highways and major roads.

Purchase your maps now at retail outlets across Ontario, or order them directly from the distributor.

General Publishing Co. Limited
325 Humber College Blvd., Etobicoke, Ontario M9W 7C3 Telephone (416) 213-1919 ext. 199
OR 1-800-387-0141 Fax (416) 213-1917

Prepayment required by cheque or credit card VISA or Mastercard.

QUANTITY				TOTAL
_____	Map #1	Southwestern Ontario	$ 7.00	_____
_____	Map #2	Lake Huron - Georgian Bay Area	$ 7.00	_____
_____	Map #3	Manitoulin Island	$ 7.00	_____
_____	Map #4	Central Ontario	$ 7.00	_____
_____	Map #5	South Central Ontario	$ 7.00	_____
_____	Map #6	Upper Ottawa Valley	$ 7.00	_____
_____	Map #7	Eastern Lake Ontario	$ 7.00	_____
_____	Map #8	Eastern Ontario	$ 7.00	_____
_____		Complete Set of 8 (for the price of seven)	$ 49.00	_____
_____		Official Road Map of Ontario	$ 2.95	_____

All prices are subject to G.S.T., P.S.T. and shipping costs. Please add 20% to your total purchase to cover taxes and shipping costs.

Sub-Total _____
Plus 20% _____
TOTAL _____

Payment by   cheque ☐   VISA ☐   Mastercard ☐

Credit Card No. _____ Expiry Date _____

Signature of Card Holder _____

SHIP TO (PLEASE PRINT):

Name: _____

Address: _____

Town/City: _____

Province: _____ Postal Code: _____

EXPRESS YOURSELF

with graphic licence plates for as low as $52.10

To order, and for more information, visit your local
Driver and Vehicle Licence Office

or **ServiceOntario Kiosk**

or call
1-800-AUTO-PL8 (1-800-288-6758)

Gift certificates available